What Others

Breaking Free from Boomerang Love:
Getting Unhooked from Borderline Personality Disorder
(*Reality Checks* is based on quotes from this book.)

As a psychotherapist dealing with borderline personality disordered people for the last 18 years, I'm thrilled to finally see a book written by a partner of BPDs for other partners.

I've served as the online therapist for the Land of Oz Internet community board (LandofOz@yahoo.groups.com) for the past five years. I've seen literally hundreds, if not thousands, of partners post on this site, begging for information and support to help them deal with the pain and confusion of their relationships with BPDs.

I'm pleased to now have *Boomerang Love* to recommend to them. It will be a lifeline to throw to them in their beaten-down despair.
— *Elyce M. Benham, MS, NCC, CCFC, LPC*

An excellent resource for someone who is caught in the cycle of violence. While not all abusers have a personality disorder, as Melville points out, the important thing is to focus on yourself, to 're-connect with yourself.' This is the only way out of an abusive relationship, since we cannot change someone else's behavior. Melville's straight-forward approach to focusing on one's self can be very helpful to anyone affected by an abusive partner.
— *Rebecca Robertson, Executive Director,*
Domestic Violence Solutions for Santa Barbara County

Thank you, thank you, *Boomerang Love!* Not knowing that I was really dealing with a personality disorder with my partner, I divorced him. I later forgave his behavior and took him back again … only to see the old painful relationship return, this time worse than before. Reading *Boomerang Love* allowed me to finally see that I could neither heal my partner, nor bear the pain of living with him, and I got out.
— *Barbara Spencer*

When I was going through the ending of my marriage, I was sure my husband was crazy … or maybe it was *I* who was the crazy one. I read *Boomerang Love* 25 years later, and so many of the behaviors I could never understand became clear to me. I wish this book had been available to me and my children at the time of my divorce from their dad. We would have been able to understand that their dad couldn't love my children or father them as they needed, because of his mental disorder. So much hurt and grief would have been avoided.

I urge anyone who is dealing with a painful, abusive relationship to read this book. The tragedy is in expecting normal behaviors from someone who is so deeply injured that they cannot function with awareness of the suffering of another.

— *Pat Haley*

Contributed Anonymously:

- Thank you for putting into words exactly what was going on in my relationship. Of all the books I've read on BPD, yours was the most informative. It gave me the strength to move on. (I'm eight months removed from a ten-year nightmare.)
- As I read your book, I felt as though I was reading a journal of my chaotic marriage with my borderline wife, except I was reading your words. Your book belongs in the office of every therapist, as it provides a rare insight into the life of a person in the difficult position of recovering from the abuse sustained in a borderline relationship.
- Though my relationship was long ago, the devastation left following the storm had left me numb to life for quite a number of years. Reading your book and then knowing that there was an actual "name to my pain" (borderline personality disorder) was like salve to my wounds, the healing element that had been missing all these years. At last I knew the "why's." Going back and re-living my pain, this time with "new eyes" that understood BPD, released those many years of pent-up pain.

Reality Checks

from Boomerang Love

Lifelines for People
Caught in Abusive Relationships

Lynn Melville

Lynn Melville
Sept. 24, 2007

Melville Publications

REALITY CHECKS
FROM BOOMERANG LOVE
LIFELINES FOR PEOPLE CAUGHT
IN ABUSIVE RELATIONSHIPS

Please note that the last name I bear now does not belong to the BPD partner I refer to in this book.

Published by
Melville Publications
PO Box 2036
Santa Maria, CA 93457-2036
Web site: www.boomeranglove.com

Printed in the United States of America

Dedication

As the second book in the *Boomerang Love* series, *Reality Checks* is an *emotional first aid kit* for readers – the book we carry in our purse or briefcase for quick booster shots of courage and empowerment when depression starts to take us down. Or the book we desperately reach for when doubts and uncertainties hit us – when the *woulda, coulda, shoulda's* begin to weaken our resolve to leave our abusive relationship.

This book is dedicated to all those people still living in relationships where they're being mistreated, where love is withheld for the slightest misstep, and where fear of punishment is a constant companion.

May this little book of verbal statements/reality snapshots and spiritual affirmations serve as crumbs on the pathway to lead you out of your forest of confusion and hopelessness. Your new life of freedom from fear, ultimately leading to happiness and joy, is waiting for you just over the next hill.

Simply hold onto *Reality Checks* and put one foot in front of the other until you get there.

The Creation of Adam

Michelangelo's *Creation of Adam* (painted in 1510, and located in the Vatican's Sistene Chapel) shown below depicts the moment when God "breathed" life into Adam.

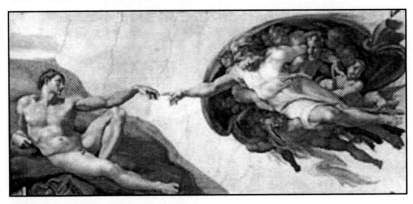

Above each affirmation in this book, I have used a close-up of the touching of their fingers to portray the help we receive when we request assistance from a higher power, whatever we perceive that to be.

The intimate touching of fingers also represents to me that very *human* potential of reaching out to bring hope and light into the darkness of another person's life and soul. Every spiritual master who has walked the face of our earth has called for us to love and care for one another. May we find the compassion and the humility to follow that direction.

About the Author

The author enjoys the company of her grandsons

In writing this book, Lynn's personal mission is to raise awareness of *boomerang love*, so that it becomes a household phrase, the meaning of which is clear to everyone.

She believes that repeatedly leaving and then returning to a painful relationship with another person is a sign that something is seriously wrong – we just haven't known what that *something* is.

Lynn has served as executive director of the Mental Health Association in her home town. Working with an all-volunteer board and community volunteers, she strived to educate people about mental health issues. She has also served on numerous charitable boards and with many non-profit organizations. She currently works as a long term care insurance agent and resides in the Central Coast region of California. For more information, see Lynn's web site at:

www.boomeranglove.com.

Other Books by Lynn Melville

Breaking Free from Boomerang Love: Getting Unhooked from Borderline Personality Disorder Relationships (2004)

Contents

Introduction

Remember Hans Christian Andersen's fairy tale of *Hansel and Gretel?* They were the children left in the forest by a weakened, beaten-down father who had been commanded by his wife (probably borderline personality disordered) to abandon their children in the forest.

The father did his best. He told his children that, from his sandwich, he'd leave a trail of crumbs in the forest, so they could find their way out. But birds ate the crumbs ... and the children were left without help.

As partners of people who mistreat us constantly (probably borderline personality disordered people), *we* live in a forest – an absolute jungle of pain, shame and despair. What we don't *know* – and can't *perceive* because of the confusion and fear we live in with our abusing partners – is that light and a new life are waiting for us right around the next corner. It's closer than we think.

We just need to take the steps to get there.

This little book provides *a trail of crumbs* on the pathway out of that painful forest, showing partners of BPDs the view of reality they need in order to regain control of their lives. These little bite-sized reality nuggets will help and inspire you to begin your climb out of the forest and over the hill to safety and peace.

Reality Checks from Boomerang Love is a powerful collection of carefully chosen excerpts from my book, *Breaking Free from Boomerang Love: Getting Unhooked from Borderline Personality Disorder Relationships*. In writing *Breaking Free from Boomerang Love*, I chronicled my own personal journey from pain to understanding, from crippling depression to exuberant expression and living life again.

To learn about borderline personality disorder, there are many resources, from doing full research on the Internet to reading my previous book, *Boomerang Love*, along with all the many other books written about BPD. *Boomerang Love*, however, is the first book written solely by a *partner* to a BPD. All the other books have been written by mental health professionals.

My website, www.boomeranglove.com, offers over 30 pages of education regarding the behavior and symptoms of BPD. I have also added a section at the end of this book entitled Definitions and Behavior Descriptions of Borderline and Narcissistic Personality Disorders. This section quotes the DSM-IV (Diagnostic and Statistical Manual), which is used by mental health professionals to understand and diagnose personality disorders.

Also at the end of this book is another section entitled *Red Flags*. This is a listing of *tip of the iceberg* behavior that might indicate more serious, underlying problems in another person – problems that could ultimately lead into a painful long term relationship.

When you have a clear picture of what borderline personality disorder *is* – what it looks like and how it acts . . .

And when you've truly *felt* those feelings that you've kept buried deep inside yourself for so long, because it seemed like there was nowhere to go with them . . .

Your heart will then know what it needs to do.

Your head has always known . . . .

Hugs for the journey,

Lynn Melville

The Graceful Exit

There's a trick to the Graceful Exit, I suspect. It begins with the vision to recognize when a job, a life stage, a relationship is over and to let go. It means leaving what's over without denying its validity or its past importance in our lives.

It involves a sense of the future, a belief that every exit line is an entry, that we are moving on, rather than out.

Some people, of course, play every scene in preparation for the end. If they don't get involved, they can easily leave – no muss, no fuss.

But those who make commitments, who attach themselves to people or roles or jobs, find it harder to disengage without a devastating loss of self. They often have to be pushed out, or they hang in there, acquiring the pallor of the dogged survivor. Or they finally leave, throwing a finger at the world.

The trick of exiting well may be the trick of living well. It's hard to recognize that life isn't a holding action, but a process. It's hard to learn that we don't leave the best parts of ourselves behind, back in the dugout or the office.

We own what we *learned* back there.

— Author unknown

REALITY CHECKS
FROM
BOOMERANG LOVE

CONFUSING, convoluted, roller coaster, stuck *boomerang* love grief. 12-Step programs call it the *Dance of Death* because it'll kill us.

WHETHER we decide to stay and ride the BPD roller coaster – or bail out and leave the relationship – the grief is the same.

We must separate from someone we love deeply. If we stay with them, we separate emotionally. If we leave, we separate from them emotionally *and* physically.

I'VE left, and he'll never rage at me again
... but I still love him. What's *wrong* with me?

WE are caught in the downward spiral of *their* illness. It's a vortex that will suck us right down with them. We are of no value to anyone – ourselves, our families or our BPD – if we allow ourselves to go down with *their* ship.

MY BPD partner presented to me the person he would have liked to have been – *not* the person he actually was.

DAY by day, I gave myself away, self-editing myself into a scared little church mouse . . . an inch at a time . . . until I no longer remembered where I put myself, or who I used to be.

UNLESS a BPD *honestly* and *actively* wants to stop destroying his life (and the others in it with him), there is absolutely no hope for a better life. Period. End of story.

GOD, open my heart so that I may trust that help is on the way. It's been such a long time coming . . . and I'm so weary.

SOMETIMES it feels as if I'm
playing a high-stakes poker game with my life.
God, give me the knowledge and courage to
know "when to hold 'em and when to fold 'em."

I'M setting firm boundaries, learning
all I can about the disorder, talking to a mental health professional for my support and
guidance, attending support groups, caring
for my physical health, and nurturing my emotional health. Doing battle with the Beast
requires careful, disciplined preparation.

GOD, help me to stay in step with my own personal journey, *walking in my own moccasins* to the beat of the drum I hear. I know I will receive guidance and comfort along the way and the strength to keep walking, wherever I am led.

LOVE is the strongest force on this earth. But sometimes even love isn't enough.

WHATEVER we compromise ourselves to get, we'll lose.

GOD, give me the strength to keep searching for answers to the pain of my partner's BPD disorder. We've all suffered long enough.

GOD, help me to see when my actions will compromise my integrity and leave me with that telltale sense of shame. I deserve to emerge from these life lessons with my dignity intact.

I'VE tried so hard to be the healer. I can stop working at it now. I can surrender to the knowledge of BPD and the freedom that it brings. In surrendering, I win back my *self*.

THE good news is, "We can relax now." We've found the answer. We've learned about BPD. We can finally let go – release – stop holding our breath.

IN surrender, I *knew* – to the core of my being – that I could do *absolutely nothing* to heal my partner. Only *my partner* could do it – *if* he wanted to.

GOD, help me to forgive myself for having walked into such a painful relationship. I went into the relationship with my *heart* wide open. Help me now to fully activate my *head* to stop blaming myself and begin taking the steps necessary to protect myself and my family.

ONCE we understand the BPD disorder, we can stop blaming ourselves for getting into a relationship that was full of so much torment and suffering.

GOD, help me to let go of my need to minimize the reality of my pain. Help me to see my situation clearly – to see *what is*. When I have the courage to admit *what is*, my eyes will be opened to a pathway of healing. Help me to be receptive to the guidance in store for me.

NO matter how hard we work to make something turn out the way we want, most of life is out of our control. We only make it harder on ourselves when we fight it.

GOD, help me keep a sense of humor about the predicament I'm in. The humorist and essayist C. W. Metcalf said, "Humor is about perspective – a willingness to access joy even in adversity."

IT'S a high-stakes poker game. With no knowledge or education about BPD, we can't win. We have no chips.

EACH piece of education about BPD I receive represents another chip on my side of the table in this high-stakes relationship game I'm playing. As the stacks grow, I'll play the game more skillfully. Ultimately, I'll know whether I want to continue playing the game – or take my chips and move on.

TURN around and face the direction the horse is going!

WITHOUT education about BPD, we're left feeling like we've been spun in a circle blindfolded and then told to *Pin the Tail on the Problem*. How do we find something that we've never known existed? It's like playing hide-and-seek with a ghost who knows all the hiding places.

DENIAL is a warm blanket we wrap around ourselves, cocooning us from the pain of knowledge of the truth about our lives.

WE are *not* responsible for *everything* that happens in this world. We didn't *cause* the BPD's behavior – we just *triggered* it. It's . . . not . . . our . . . fault.

TO a BPD, a relationship is sometimes just a contract . . . a *cancelable* one . . . at their control and whim.

GOD, I didn't *cause* this disorder, I can't *control* it, and I certainly can't *cure* it. Help me stop beating myself up about something over which I have *absolutely no control.*

GOD, help me to remember that my BPD partner is ill, but I can't save him from the results of his actions. Help me get off his back, out of his way, and on with my life.

No matter how many times we're told by outside parties that we're not to blame for our BPD's behavior, it's hard not to accept those accusations when they're hurled at us like swords. Both parties (the BPD and their partner) are groping in the dark, looking for a way out of the pain. The problem is: *both parties blame the same person – us!*

TRYING to stop a raging BPD is like throwing feathers at a stampeding rhinoceros.

BPD is a mental disorder, and we cannot change the misfiring signals of their brains or give them the chemicals they need to stop the overreactions. We're not capable of re-programming them, no matter how much we believe *love* will do it.

OUR task is to get out of our BPD's way and let the consequences of their actions happen to them . . . *without* putting a pillow under their tush when they hit bottom.

ALL things change, end, move on. I don't know what the future holds for me with my BPD, but my goal is to be a whole person when the dust settles – not road kill.

ULTIMATELY, we *are* in control of ourselves, even with a BPD partner. If we weren't, it wouldn't be possible for *anyone* to ever get better, ourselves included.

MY self, my soul and my spirit yearn for peace and serenity, love and warmth. I, too, have a journey on this earth and much to accomplish. I *resolve* to lock hands with other partners of BPDs, walk through the pain and the lessons, and get to the other side. Love and light await me.

I don't have to go it alone anymore, hanging my head in shame and humiliation. There are mental health therapists now who are trained to help the BPD and their partner. I just need to find the courage to admit the pain in my life and ask for help. Help is there for the asking now.

I am an absolute, scared-out-of-my-mind, quacking, *sitting duck* for someone who uses anger to intimidate and manipulate others to get their way. If I don't have the strength to stand up to these people, then I need to make *darned* sure I don't let them into my life.

GOD, help me to surround myself with *safe* people. People who scare me with their anger will cause me to self-sabotage with people-pleasing behavior again. I've waited so long to feel safe.

WE can't know everything about how the future will work out. We can hand it over to a power greater than ourselves (God) to handle for us ... and then go do the laundry.

THERE'S a balance and an order to our lives that we can only see when looking backwards. Whether we stay in the relationship with our BPD or not, we can have faith that we will be guided on that path. We will be provided with the answers when we need them.

SLEEPWALKING through our lives by allowing denial or minimizing to slip into our perceptions will only lead us to more pain. Staying alert to whether or not the hurtful behavior is truly diminishing is *crucial.* It's information we need in order to make decisions in *our* lives for *ourselves.*

THE choices our BPD partners make in *their* lives also have consequences in *our* lives. Losing our love may be the price they have to pay for their lack of honesty, humility and courage.

GOD, help me to know clearly that no one can abandon me any more, because I've become an adult. I can take care of myself now.

EDUCATION about BPD acts as a shield about us and deflects the pain from the blaming, projection and rage of the BPD ... or at least the hurt doesn't penetrate in as far. With practice and more education, we can learn not to let it in at all.

HAVING possibly chosen my BPD partner to make up for the losses of my childhood, it's sometimes very difficult to have common sense in my *today* moments. Sometimes it seems as if the grieving of my *yesterdays* threatens to drown my *todays*.

SOMETIMES it feels like I'm walking on red hot coals . . . in my bare feet . . . blindfolded.

THE knowledge regarding BPD and the tools to cope with it are becoming known. We tell one person, who tells another, who tells another. Holding hands, sharing our experience, strength and hope, a circle of changed lives will slowly encompass our world.

THE more crap you put up with, the more crap you'll get.

BPDs project their feelings onto *us* – and then get hurt and mad at *us* because they think *we* have those feelings. They re-create *us* in their minds as *their* persecutor – with *their* projections.

ULTIMATELY, if the hurtful BPD behavior continues with no movement toward treatment, we have a hard decision to make. Would we like to fly on the Hindenburg or take the Titanic – stay or leave the relationship? Either choice has its pain, but the decision to leave at least has a chance to stop the pain some time in the future.

DOWN the hall are all these doors. You knock on the doors, and the door that opens, you go in. The door that stays closed, you're not to go in.

EVERYTHING I ever let go of had claw marks all over it.

I am loved because I have so deeply given love first. The fact that the quality of my love hasn't been returned to me by my BPD partner in the same way I gave it is not my fault.

OUR personal backgrounds created enormous capacities for empathy, sympathy, love and forgiveness. Because of this, we not only are able to give the intensity of love a BPD needs so desperately, but we're also easy to manipulate.

As a result of their early childhood losses, BPDs search carefully for their partners, cautiously measuring personality qualities and choosing people with whom they feel the most loved – and, more importantly, with whom they feel the most confidence that they won't be *abandoned*.

As my BPD partner works on healing and not using manipulation on me, help me, in turn, learn to be not so *easily manipulated*.

GOD, help me find the words to show the love and acceptance I have in my heart for my partner, but also deliver the message that I am *not* responsible for his feelings or actions.

WE *know* the disorder of BPD is there, because the way they act clearly isn't normal. We just can't *see* the disorder, because we haven't known its *name*.

THE truth is that I was caught in a subconscious ritual of behavior I'd learned in my childhood. I placated anger (out of fear), people-pleased (again out of fear), and was easily manipulated by love withdrawal and threats of abandonment (did I mention fear?).

THERE is such a sense of confusion in a relationship with a BPD, because they're not always the *same person*. We know the good person we fell in love with, but who in the world is this raging beast who appears every once in a while and causes great hurt?

So we release our BPDs. We send them along with as much forgiveness as we can muster at that point in *our* healing. We wish them courage and strength for the lessons that life will be showing them, now that we're not protecting and rescuing them *from* those lessons.

WE reach pity and then forgiveness for our BPD partners when we truly see the depth of their illness – the brokenness, the desperation, the hell hole they live in.

KNOWLEDGE about BPD came to my rescue. It became like a sport for me. Whenever I'd feel myself slipping back to old hurts and angers, I would re-read about the disorder, its causes and behaviors. That somehow helped me de-personalize the pain and pull me out of it.

SOME of us hang onto our anger because it's the only way we can give ourselves any sense of power. The splitting/devaluation acted out on us leaves us feeling so power-*less*.

I am entirely ready to begin gently and lovingly caring for *myself*, whether my BPD partner begins work on his *own* recovery or not.

WE don't realize we're wearing an emotional hair shirt until we take it off – it feels so good to relax and not scratch all the time.

WE sooner or later may have to face the reality that a close, intimate relationship may never be available with our BPDs – they may never get well enough to be a kind, loving partner for us.

WE need to learn to give the same level of love and nurture to ourselves that we've been giving to our BPD.

WHEN we want a certain result, we should make sure that result is available in the situation. A friend of mine likes to say, "You can't get orange juice from a door knob."

GOD, help me to remember that new ways of thinking and acting take time and energy to learn. Help me to withhold judgment as my BPD partner struggles to restrain himself with more effective cognitive and life skills.

GOD, help me to remember when I'm slipping into depression and self-pity that things could be much, much worse. I could still be one of those millions of people who still don't know the *name of their pain*.

I know I can't be abandoned any more. I'm an adult now.

WE'RE all adults now. Knowing we were *conditioned* as children to respond in fear, we no longer need to be enslaved by it. There are no victims – only subconsciously pre-programmed volunteers.

GOD, help me to face the reality of how my childhood experiences formed me into the Perfect BPD Partner. Help me learn not to be so easily manipulated.

AS children, when we were raged at or ignored in silence, we felt scared, alone and abandoned.

We scurried to do whatever we could to get the love of our parent back. We were sad little children with a very unhealthy *learned* way of responding to manipulation now permanently installed in our software.

NOW that I have the knowledge I've needed all along about BPD, I can make better choices. When I know better, I do better.

WE feel like the strawman in *The Wizard of Oz*. The monkeys who fly out of trees have pulled all our insides out, and they're strewn everywhere. Limp and sad, our body sits by the side of the road, trying to figure out how to get our life and our personhood back. We need re-stuffing . . . and re-stuffing takes time.

WE are trusting, good people who've been run over by a disguised, punishing, out-of-control tank. If we'd known it was coming, we certainly would have gotten out of its way.

ALL control is really in the hands of our BPD partners. Try as we might, we can't see inside their heads to know what's *really* going on in there, to protect ourselves in advance of their actions. I wonder if we'll ever *really* be safe . . . I wonder . . . .

HOW do we hide when the inescapable feeling of having been played for a fool washes over us? We're like Charlie Brown in the *Peanuts* cartoon – we trusted that she wouldn't do it, but Lucy tricked us with the football again.

GOD, help me to be aware of the subtle signs that I may possibly be blindly walking into yet another BPD relationship. Help me to see what I need to see and *hear* what I need to hear. I don't ever want to hurt that bad again.

UNLESS we use the knowledge we've gained about BPD to carefully evaluate the people we allow into our lives, we're almost doomed to continue getting ensnared in the quicksand of BPD-ism over and over again. As one of my friends says, "I've been married to the same man for 20 years – just different names."

IF we fold and go back to old behaviors to save a BPD relationship (for now), we need to go easy on ourselves, to be gentle in our self-judgment. We're not strong enough yet to handle the relationship ending. These types of relationships aren't over until they're over . . . and it takes as many times as it takes.

I *must* survive this BPD relationship so I can go on to help the others who still don't know the *name of their pain* or how to protect themselves from it.

TRULY, we *are* heroes, as we work to balance supporting our BPD's efforts to recover with *our* need for safety. But when is enough enough? By what sign will we know that it's time to throw in the towel? The difficult question for *us* is: At what point do we stop being heroes and turn into martyrs?

CO-DEPENDENTS Anonymous says some of us *stay in harmful jobs and relationships far too long.* For me, I can only see *far too long* looking backwards. Looking forwards is more complicated . . . .

GOD, if I'm starting to lose my openness and ability to reach out in love to the world around me, perhaps it's time for a reality check regarding how my BPD relationship is affecting me. Help me to perceive my life without denial or minimizing. Help me to know when it's time to leave.

THE Wizard of Oz to the Cowardly Lion: "As for you, my friend, you are a victim of disorganized thinking. You are under the unfortunate delusion that simply because you run away from danger, you have no courage. You are confusing courage with wisdom."

WE *must* survive our BPD relationship. Our mission, when we get *our* lives in order, is to move on to help those who still don't know the *name of their pain.* There are *so* many others who need our help . . . they may not make it without us.

IF we're halfway up the sides of the pit on our way out of our BPD relationship, it's important not to look down . . . or look back. We might be tempted to try to help just one more time . . . .

IT doesn't matter that we don't *deserve* it. It doesn't matter that we didn't *cause* it. And it doesn't matter that we're bright, capable, loving people, either. What *does* matter is that to everyone looking *into* our lives, all they see is a shambles – a soap opera of emotional drama that makes absolutely no sense at all and leaves *us* looking like fools.

IT seems to me that our struggle as partners of BPDs is that we will always love the *mask* – the person they initially presented to us, the one we fell in love with. It's hard to accept the reality of who the BPD really *is* – that the mask doesn't actually exist. The mask is just the person our BPD partners *wish* they could be.

COMBINING fear with kindness is such a powerful tool to *cripple a person psychologically* that the military trains its personnel in how to resist it. It's a psychological warfare tool used in concentration and prisoner-of-war camps. When our BPD acts lovingly to us and then is cruel, our relationship has become a psychological concentration camp.

IF my BPD partner isn't going to do *his* part, it's entirely up to me. I may be digging out with a spoon, but eventually, I *will* get out.

WHEN our BPD relationships end, sometimes with brutal pain, we feel like we are totally alone in a sea of grief. No one understands the suffering and emotional damage of being in a relationship with a BPD. So no one can grieve with us – or even walk along with us emotionally.

CLOSURE after the ending of a relationship with a BPD? Where do we put the love we had (and still might have) for the good part of our BPD? A death really *has* occurred.

The knowledge of the existence of BPD forces an acceptance of the death of the person we *thought* they were – and therefore, our *love* for the good part that we *thought* our BPD possessed must die also. We're grieving the *death* of a person who continues to walk and talk in a physical form around us, still pretending to be the good person we fell in love with.

It's the most convoluted, twisted form of grieving we'll ever experience.

GOD, help me to hold my head high and not feel ashamed of how my life has become such an embarrassing experience. At least now I know the truth and the *name of my pain*. I can now begin putting the pieces of my life back together again.

MOST BPDs reveal their hurtful behaviors very slowly. They emerge gradually, over time. During that process, we become so conditioned to the behaviors that they seem *normal* to us. And so we learn to accept the unacceptable.

WHAT do *you* need to do to start healing from your BPD relationship? Music? Art? Dancing? Walk on the beach? Whatever it is, find a way to start doing it ... today. If we don't start our *own* healing, the disorder of BPD will have claimed *two* lives instead of one.

WHAT most people don't understand is that the person we made our commitment to is *not* the person we eventually ended up with.

WE can end up after one of these BPD relationships with our own form of intimacy fear – like a disease we caught from our BPD partner. We wall ourselves off physically and emotionally from others. Sometimes we hide ourselves so well we forget where we put ourselves.

GOD, give me courage as I take my first baby steps in learning to stand up for myself. Help my head to overcome my demon fears and my overly forgiving heart.

AS my faith in a force greater than myself (for me, that is God) became stronger, as He acted in my life to care for me (new friends, new jobs, wonderful new opportunities), I began to not feel so alone. I could finally say, "No," to a relationship where someone was hurting me and walk away.

MY *head* is strong enough now to out-wrestle my fearful heart and make healthy choices as to who I will *allow* in my life – and who I will *not.*

ARE you still feeling the pain and depression from the craziness you've been living in with your BPD? Stay with the feelings and let them wash over you. At the end of that deep intensity, you'll find your backbone of steel that says, "I will *not* be treated this way any longer. Nor will I allow my children to be treated in this manner or any longer raised in this environment."

BEHAVIOR based on fear of abandonment will *sabotage* our lives.

RELATIONSHIPS – good or bad – are opportunities to truly know and *experience* Who We Are. How can we know how loving we are if no one needs our love? How can we know how honest we are if no one gives us the opportunity to cheat? And how can we know how strong we are if no one tries to overpower us?

I know now that emotional pain is an indicator that something is wrong in my life – that something needs attention, not denial, not running away from it. Forcing myself to stop and figure out *where* the pain is coming from allows me to decide what *action* needs to be taken to *stop* the pain.

SOMEDAY you'll know – to the core of your being – that you're someone worthy of love that doesn't leave or punish ... and you'll start dreaming of how to get that kind of love in your life. Dreaming is the first step to obtaining.

Reality Ticklers
from
Boomerang Love

WELCOME to the club for People Who Had Too Much Patience.

LAST words from a BPD in a divorce: "I'm *not* a BPD! You just didn't give me enough attention!"

EVENTUALLY you come to realize that there was *no* reason to consider the feelings of someone who just *hurt* you continually.

IF my BPD was doing *physical* harm, the abuse would be obvious. But if we're *emotionally* abused, then first we have to explain it to them and why it's wrong. There is something insidious about being hurt and having to explain *why* we hurt, because someone else's view of reality is so distorted.

CO-DEPENDENCY issues are self-denial issues – "You can do anything to me as long as you love me."

SOME really smart people grow up and just *live in their heads*. It's easier not to feel pain that way . . . .

IT'S very easy to confuse compassion with co-dependency.

PERSONALITY disorders are like one-armed bandits in a casino. We keep putting money in, expecting a pay-out. The machine flashes its lights, states the current jackpot and generally looks like a payment is coming. We may get small payments, but we never get the jackpot. The purpose of the flashing lights and small payouts is to ensure that we keep putting our coins in.

ULTIMATUMS are not obligations.

IN my relationship with my BPD, I felt like I'd been torn apart, piece by piece, as if I'd been kidnapped from life. I can feel again now – and laugh.

BPDs can often be bright and intelligent and appear warm, friendly and competent. Sometimes they can maintain this appearance for years, until their defense structure crumbles. This usually happens around a stressful situation, such as the break-up of a romantic relationship, death of a parent, or serious illness.

THE anger and rage that is so absolutely justifiable – and has to be *felt* when your life has been ravaged by a BPD – also has to find an end.

COMEDY and real humor are not about hurting but about saving. Humor is the refuge of the powerless. The jokes about BPD reflect the powerlessness some of us feel in the face of that condition and the deep, deep sorrow.

BPD relationships are *intense* but stormy and unstable. The intensity of what I *thought* was love in the relationship was what kept me yearning for so long in my healing process.

OUR task: To attend fully to how things *are* in the present moment – and not to how things *could be* or *once were*.

JUMPING through hoops to keep
the BPD from withdrawing – or to bring them
out of withdrawal: the *devotion test* to *prove*
our love for them.

GIVE your energy to a BPD
and you give it away.

B-I-T-C-H: Babe In Total Control of Herself.

LEAVING a BPD relationship: nominee for the *Cold Turkey* poster kid award.

I'M pretty much the same *giver* that I always was. I'm not nearly as good being with a *taker* as I used to be, though.

FORGIVENESS is needed, but forgetting isn't. Otherwise, how would we ever learn? The past can be an omen of what is to come, unless true change is the focus.

IF you are co-dependent on a desert island where there is no one there to take advantage of you, are you still co-dependent?

IT takes a turning point to free oneself from hate, prejudice and love.

DREAMS and nightmares must be fed to be kept alive.

HE was like this before I met him, he was like this during our time together, and he'll be like this *long* after I'm gone. It has *nothing* to do with me.

IF it doesn't come out in the wash, it'll come out in the rinse.

THE abuse situation with a BPD is hard to see (compared to physical abuse) because of the gaslighting, constant rearranging of facts, and the cyclical nature of the *I love you so much* statements.

TO forgive or not to forgive – the key is education and understanding. Once we understand how deeply injured the BPD is, the scars from the hurt begin to fade ... replaced with something that feels like pity.

PATHOLOGICAL BPD-ism leads to dependence rather than to interdependence, to conflict rather than to collaboration, to sadistic behaviors rather than to tender emotions.
It is a malignant form of BPD-ism, because it takes over the host and then kills it.

BPDs are all actors, and we are the stage they walk on.

A pattern of impulsive flight or *retribution* (punishment) exists in situations where the BPD feels anxious and can't cope.

NEVER try to teach a pig to sing. It's a waste of time, and it annoys the pig.
— Mark Twain

DON'T be an *N-abler.*

DO not throw your pearls before swine, lest they trample them under their feet, and turn and tear you to pieces.
— New American Standard Bible, Matthew 7:6

ONCE you accept an idea, it's an idea whose time has come.

BPD-ism: the counterfeit human.

THE BPD frequently cannot and will not change. They truly, deep down, do not, and never will, believe there is anything wrong with them.

A BPD evidences resistance to the control of someone else's love for them – they feel controlled when someone loves them !

IF you do not know what direction to take, you have not acknowledged where you are.

BPDs have failed to develop the affection bonds which would allow them to empathize with another's pain.

BECOME an *uncooperative* doormat – someone unwilling to be manipulated.

FROM a partner of a BPD: "It's good to know he's in recovery, because then my own experience doesn't seem like such a waste of life."

YOU have had more than enough creepiness in your life. That part's over.

KEEP swimming to freedom and healing. You're in the middle of the lake now. If you stop, you'll drown.

ONCE you realize you have given your power away, you can make the decision to take it back.

A big day in my life was when I decided I needed to be *proactive* instead of *reactive* about this relationship and my own life.

ALL I wanted was someone to grow old with. What I got instead was someone help-ing me to an early grave.

LIVING with a BPD is like psychological incarceration – a prisoner of war camp in your own home.

IT'S difficult to accept the pain of loving someone who cannot love you, no matter what you do.

TREATING post traumatic stress disorder is difficult when the trauma isn't *past*. It's hard to get well from your hammer wounds when you're still being hit on the head.

WHAT you are afraid to do is a clear indicator of the next thing to do.

I was so dense, and so hoovered, and so committed ... to something that just wasn't there.

SOME days I'm bursting with outrage, stung with the bitter, unfair circumstances. Still other days, I am grieving as though someone has died. I have never known such melancholy.

MY BPD alternates between denial and despair.

GREEK metaphor for BPD – Trojan horse.

HUMAN development progresses in stages. Each time we were unable to resolve the tasks of one developmental stage, those of the next become even more insurmountable. Thus, BPDs are left disabled in many ways.

ULTIMATELY, you have no choice but to feel what you are feeling.

FALLING out of love is the hardest thing you'll ever do.

A BPD is limbically challenged. (The limbic system in the brain governs emotions. Medications can calm the limbic system down and reduce the BPD's overreactions.)

BPD's self-commentary: "I'm better in the abstract."

KNOWING about BPD-ism involves a loss of innocence, but it is an essential tool in navigating through society and life.

LIFE with a BPD can be either a merry-go-round or a roller coaster. With better understanding, we can get off the merry-go-round and move to a roller coaster. At least then there will be a sense of progress.

IF someone shows you who they are by their actions, *believe* them – the *first* time!

BPD-ism: a thought disorder
with transitory psychotic episodes.

THINGS are not what they
seem – they are what they are.

BPDs don't have friends –
they have prisoners.

LIFE with a BPD – soul rape.

I stayed with him and went back with him because I believe in working things out whenever possible. I was also without adequate knowledge to make a choice. When I obtained the knowledge I needed to see it for what it was, I made a firm decision and stuck with it. End of story.

PROJECTION – *you're* the one with *my* problem.

FATE is the vengeance of choices unmade.

REACTIONS of normal people (having grown up in a loving home) to BPD behavior are shock, *profound* hurt and disorientation. They then leave the relationship.

WHATEVER you are trying to avoid won't go away until you confront it.

BPDs are emotionally numb, which functions for them as emotional self-preservation.

THERE are no mistakes – only lessons.

BPDs are chronically discontent and assume the role of the *Avenger*.

IF you worry about what *might be,* and wonder what *might have been,* you will ignore what *is.*

HOW crazy craziness makes everyone, how irrationally afraid. The madness hidden in each of us, called to, identified, aroused like a lust. And against that the jaw sets. The more I fear my own insanity, the more I must punish yours.

— Kate Millett

CO-DEPENDENCE is an illness of blind denial and self-abandonment.

BEFORE I met my BPD partner, people called me *Mary Sunshine.*

ROADKILL stage of the BPD partner – emotionally flattened, feeling dead and repulsive to the world.

MANY of us are stuck in *conditional* love, which usually doesn't last and is rather manipulative.

NARCISSISM is the mental epidemic of the 20th century, a plague to be fought by all means.

— Dr. Sam Vaknin

EDUCATE people to beware of narcissists. Teach them how to identify narcissists, how to cope with them, how to avoid them, and how to divorce them.

— Dr. Sam Vaknin (www.geocoties.com/vaksam)

TO a BPD, it's the innocent and trusting people who are ideal prey.

CO-DEPENDENTS – people who see potential in others and want to encourage it.

THE rates of patient drop-out are high in trials of drugs to combat BPD behavior and thinking. Unless they become really ill, hit a wall and/or hit bottom, they just don't believe they're ill. They use blame and projection and don't see a reason to tolerate side effects of medications.

BPDs use behavior and gestures to *act* emotional – but there is no emotional correlate, no inner resonance to go along with the behavior and gestures.

BEING hoovered can feel good –
but it has consequences that *don't* feel good.

BEFORE you can break out of prison,
you must first realize you are locked up.

MOST BPDs are *stuck*
at the developmental age of two.

A few days of bliss,
followed by the days from hell.

A veil has been lifted for the first
time in my life. A crazy and confusing
existence is finally illuminated. I get it.
I understand BPD.

I'VE spent 50 years trying to
figure out why there was so much pain
in my marriage. Now I know I wasn't the
crazy one.

NOW there is a name for the monster, and I understand the fundamental dynamics.

I'VE tried and tried for so long to find happiness in my relationship. I feel like I've been digging for a golden horseshoe in a pile of horse puckey.

I'M tired of going into the corner to lick my wounds every time my BPD partner acts up or gives me the silent treatment.

SHE has split images of you, based on whether or not her needs are getting met the way she wants them.

WHEN you live with a BPD, every day is Groundhog Day. We live the same conflicts over and over, just inserting a new trigger issue every so often to give the illusion of variety.

IF it was always my fault, now that I'm gone, whose fault is it now?

I'M finally in a place where I understand that she *has* to rage, and she *deserves* to rage. I just won't *engage* her in her rage any more.

MANY of us may be too objective for our own good. I try *so* hard to see the other side and *understand.*

Well, I have just *understood* myself right into the depths of hell.

WHATEVER you are willing to put up with is exactly what you will have.

LIFE can be so good and exciting when you don't have to live each day expending all your energy on a damaged person.

"THE permanent temptation of life is to confuse dreams with reality. The permanent defeat of life comes when dreams are surrendered to reality."

— James Michener, author

TO forgive is divine . . . to forget would be stupid.

GETTING the rage out after a relationship with a BPD is like hurling. Since the partner of the BPD has swallowed so many putdowns, so much rage and sarcasm over time, it's hard to be *logical* when hurling it all back up.

A GOOD marriage is like getting to start heaven a little early.

A BPD cannot bear shame. They need an *object of scorn* to be the shame-assigned. High-functioning BPDs can be very successful in the outside world and absolute tyrants at home, because they can't handle the intimate relationship that a home life requires.

HURT people hurt people.

HARBORING resentment is like drinking poison and expecting the other person to die.

I CAN'T choose how I *feel* – but I can choose what I *do* about it.

NOW I control where I put my energy, and it's not into my BPD partner's problems. It's into my own concerns, making my own life better each day.

OUR response to life's difficulties defines who we are.

"IF one throws salt at thee, thou wilt receive no harm unless thou has sore places."
— Latin proverb

MY BPD partner was like an ever-retreating goal post in his expectations of me.

"ONE of God's greatest lessons we have to learn is about the bridges we should cross and the bridges we should burn."
— David Russell

IN a relationship with a BPD, we become *the afflicted by the afflicted.*

YOU can't negotiate with an untreated mental disorder.

BPDs use *emotional reasoning* – "I *feel* this way, so there must be facts to justify it."

P T S D: *Present* T raumatic S tress D isorder

IF you can't control it,
don't let it control you.

LOVE and forgiveness
won't cure BPD. They're like
band-aids. They help things for a
while, but then things go back to
normal – bad.

BEAUTY may be only skin deep,
but ugly goes clear through.

"FRANKLY, Scarlett, I don't give a damn."
— Rhett Butler in the movie
Gone with the Wind

I'M learning to deal with issues in
a more simple way. In this world, I've
learned that there are things that work
and things that don't work. The trick is
to stop doing the things that don't work
and start doing the things that work.

MY relationship with my BPD
partner was like a bad dance. No matter
what I did, I was never on the right foot.

WHEN you blame others,
you give up your power to change.

THE symptoms of BPD are so simi-
lar that it seems as if there are really only two
people with BPD – a male and a female – cloned
over and over in all our relationships. We're all in
BPD relationships with the same person.

THERE'S a difference between
unconditional love and blind, insane tolerance of
poor treatment.

A friend asked me if he would still be my friend if he had treated me the way my BPD partner did. I replied that I wouldn't have considered him much of a friend. He said, "Just my point."

DIVORCES are final long before they go to court.

JOURNALS can be good reality tests. Read the awful parts every time you're tempted to get sucked back in. Repeat the following frequently: "This behavior is *not* normal," "This abuse is *not* okay," and "I deserve my own boundaries, emotions, thoughts and happiness."

IT takes a long time for burns to heal,
whether they're outside or inside.

WE'RE *objects* that *should* meet their
needs. When we don't do that, then we're split into
those *all bad objects* and punished.

THE more difficult tasks in life are
that way because the reward at the end is that
much more precious.

BPDs are people known by the place in their brain that's not working properly.

PERSONALITY disorders (PDs), by definition, are disorders of personality.

Consequently, they are typified by early onset, pervasive effects, and relatively poor prognosis – it's hard to cure someone of their personality. Nevertheless, there *are* treatments that can help those with PDs learn to cope with their distinctive problems in living.

MY partner is BPD and OCD, with psychotic tendencies – which is the gift that keeps on giving.

THE one who loves the least controls the relationship.

I knew that I would always have love for my partner. However, there were parts of my life that I *could* not, *dared* not, open to her again, not only because of the pain it would cause me, but because she could not handle those parts – and I could not live without them.

THE Good Witch in the movie *The Wizard of Oz:* "You've had the power all along."

MY land is bare of chattering folk;
The clouds are low along the ridges,
And sweet's the air with curly smoke,
From all my burning bridges.
— Dorothy Parker

THE BPD feels like a *victim* (powerless). They may try to overcompensate for this by attempting to control others, only to find that they can't, which can substantiate that they *don't* have control . . . in which case they punish.

AERODYNAMICALLY, the bumblebee shouldn't be able to fly, but the bumblebee doesn't know that, so it goes on flying anyway.
— Mary Kay Ash, founder of Mary Kay Cosmetics

THOUGH we travel the world over to find the beautiful, we must carry it with us or we will find it not.

— Ralph Waldo Emerson

BE true to yourself, do what is in your heart, love your BPD partner with everything you have. But know when to say when . . . because sometimes that which has not killed us just wasn't given enough time.

IF you board the wrong train, it's no use running along the corridor in the other direction.

AFFIRMATIONS
FROM
BOOMERANG LOVE

GOD, FOR TODAY help me to control my boomerang love. Help me to step over, walk around, punch my way through my grief and take care of myself in whatever way I must. And help me tomorrow, next week, next month, and next year.

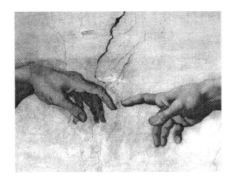

GOD, FOR TODAY give me the strength to keep searching for answers, whether I stay with my BPD partner or not. Lead me to therapists who truly understand and can diagnose and treat BPD. Help me find those therapists who also understand the living hell created by this disorder for me, my partner and our family. We've all suffered long enough.

Open my heart so that I may trust that help is on the way. It's been such a long time coming ... and I'm so weary.

GOD, FOR TODAY, help me to clearly see the direction in which my life is moving. Help me have faith in *progress, not perfection* in my healing journey. Keep me alert to the signposts along the way which tell me if progress is truly occurring with my BPD.

Sometimes it feels as if I'm playing a high stakes poker game with my life. Give me the knowledge and courage to know *when to hold 'em and when to fold 'em.*

GOD, FOR TODAY, guide me to the people who can comfort and support me as I struggle with this terribly destructive disorder. I want to finish the grief and begin my life dance again.

GOD, FOR TODAY, help me to remember that everyone is on a journey of learning and awareness here on this earth. Some of us have been thrust further ahead than others because of the circumstances in our lives. Therefore, we "walk to a different drummer."

Help me to stay in step with my journey, walking in my moccasins to the beat of the drum *I* hear. I know I will receive guidance and comfort along the way and the strength to keep walking, wherever I am being led.

GOD, FOR TODAY, help me to fight the beaten-down, worn-out feeling that comes over me each time I am blamed and raged at for the feelings of my partner. I didn't *cause* them – I only *triggered* them.

Give me strength to nurture myself, one step at a time, until I am strong enough to take larger actions, speak with a louder voice, and erect psychological barriers so I am not hurting so badly.

My self, my soul and my spirit yearn for peace and serenity, love and warmth. I must protect them so they don't die too early, leaving me walking around like a shell, hollow inside.

I, too, have a journey on this earth and much to accomplish.

I *resolve* to lock hands with other partners of BPDs, walk through the pain and the lessons, and get to the other side.

Love and light await me.

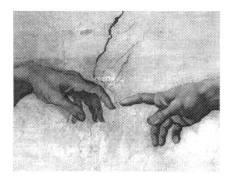

God, FOR TODAY, I know that I'm not alone in my journey of self-strengthening and taking back my power. I am eager to receive Your comfort and guidance as the steps on my pathway unfold. I do not want to live in a burning corral forever.

GOD, FOR TODAY, help me to walk the tightrope of my relationship, giving support where it's needed, love when it's accepted. Help me to see when my actions will compromise my integrity and leave me with that telltale sense of shame. I deserve to emerge from these life lessons with my dignity intact.

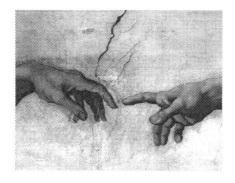

GOD, FOR TODAY, help me to turn my partner over to you for recovery. I've tried so hard to be the healer. I can stop working at it now. I can surrender to the knowledge of BPD and the freedom that brings. In surrendering, I win back my "self."

GOD, FOR TODAY, help me to forgive myself for having walked into such a painful relationship. I know there's a very good part to my partner, and that's the person I love. I have beaten myself up inside mercilessly for having made what looks like such a stupid mistake.

I went into the relationship with my *heart* wide open. Help me now to fully activate my *head* to stop blaming myself and begin taking the steps necessary to protect myself and my family.

GOD, FOR TODAY, help me to let go of my need to minimize the reality of my pain. Help me to see my situation clearly – to see *what is*. I know that when I have the courage to admit *what is*, my eyes will be opened to a pathway of healing, one step at a time. Help me be receptive to the guidance in store for me.

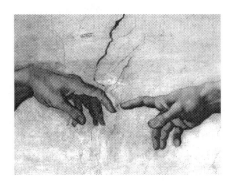

GOD, FOR TODAY, help me keep a sense of humor about the predicament I'm in.

The humorist and essayist C. W. Metcalf said, "Humor is about perspective – a willingness to access joy even in adversity."

GOD, FOR TODAY, help me to listen to the quiet voice inside me which is offering comfort and guidance through all the noise and confusion of my life. Give me the ears to hear ... the eyes to see ... and the courage to follow through.

I must remember that *I* am the *most valuable dog.*

GOD, FOR TODAY, give me the courage to stop denying the reality of what I'm living with and the willingness to accept my place at the poker table. I know that acceptance is the key to the action of acquiring knowledge about BPD.

Each piece of education I receive represents another poker chip on my side of the table. As the stacks grow, I'll play the game more skillfully.

Ultimately, I'll know whether I want to continue playing the game – or take my chips and move on.

GOD, FOR TODAY, help me not be so hard on myself. Help me not be so quick to take the blame when my BPD rages. I am *not* responsible for *everything* that happens in this world.

GOD, FOR TODAY, help me to choose wisely in my relationships next time ... if there *is* a next time. Guide me to a relationship where I am free to be myself, warts and all – a relationship where I'm free to have a *time out* of giving (during a physical illness, a deep grieving over the death of a loved one) without being punished.

I want a relationship where my partner is able to step forward in *my* time of need to lovingly care for *me*. I am a good, caring person. I deserve to receive the kind of love that I offer.

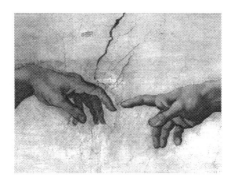

GOD, FOR TODAY, help me to remember that *I* didn't cause this disorder (may those who *did* cause it suffer an equal consequence, thank you very much). I can't control it (trying to stop a raging BPD is like throwing feathers at a stampeding rhinoceros). And *I* certainly can't cure it (although *they* can work at controlling it – and recovering from it – if they *choose*).

Help me to stop beating myself up about something over which I have *absolutely no control.*

GOD, FOR TODAY, help me to accept that I can't change anyone. Help me to remember that advice or help not asked for is usually not taken. Show me how to accept myself as I am … impossible wishes, dreams and all.

I promise to keep taking care of myself by setting clear boundaries with my BPD. I know that all things change, end, move on – as will my BPD relationship. I don't know what the future holds, but my goal is to be a whole person when the dust settles – not road-kill.

GOD, FOR TODAY, help me to think clearly. What would I do if my partner had a heart condition yet still ate fatty foods and wouldn't exercise?

How would I react if he had diabetes and wouldn't stop eating sugar? Eventually, I'd have to get out of his way and let the consequences of his actions happen to him ... *without* putting a pillow under his tush when he hits bottom.

Help me to remember that my partner is ill, but I can't save him from the results of his actions. If he continues to do the actions which I have said will have consequences to them, give me the strength to follow through on those consequences.

Help me to get off his back, out of his way, and on with my life.

GOD, FOR TODAY, help me remember that my first responsibility is to myself. I *must* survive this. I must protect my children. I must figure out how I got into a relationship like this ... and find a way to survive it or get out of it ... with my sanity and body intact.

Mending my heart, soul and spirit will take a little longer.

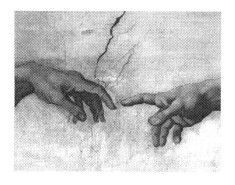

GOD, FOR TODAY, help me to know that I don't have to go it alone anymore … hanging my head in shame and humiliation, accepting blame that isn't mine. Give me the courage to step forward, admit the pain in my life, and ask for help. It's there for the asking now.

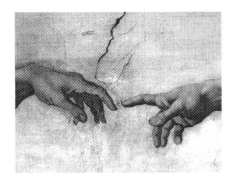

GOD, FOR TODAY, help me to surround myself with *safe* people – friends, acquaintances, work environments, bosses, family members and especially lovers and spouses. People who scare me will endanger my "sobriety" (will cause me to people-please), my sanity and my very physical well-being. They'll lure me to drink of the cup of self-sabotaging fear again. I don't want to slip again.

I've waited so long to feel safe. I don't want my life to be a *mess* ever again.

God, for today, help me to silence my fears and anxieties. I know that the disorder of BPD took many years to form and that it won't go away overnight. I ask for wisdom to know what I need to do to protect myself and my family and to help my BPD. And most of all, I ask for *strength* to carry out those actions.

GOD, FOR TODAY, I ask for the courage and strength to hold up against the BPD onslaught when I am split "all bad." Help me find ways to protect myself as the healing and recovery process continues with my partner.

GOD, FOR TODAY, help me to keep the pain of my "inner child" under control so I can see my situation clearly. Having possibly chosen my BPD partner to make up for the losses of my childhood, it's sometimes very difficult to have common sense in my *today* moments. Sometimes it seems as if the grieving of my *yesterdays* threatens to drown my *todays*.

Help me to know clearly that no one can abandon me any more, because I've become an adult. I can take care of myself now.

GOD, FOR TODAY, help me to honestly absorb all the information I need in order to take care of myself. Sometimes it feels like I'm walking on red hot coals ... in my bare feet ... blind-folded. I am grateful for all that I've learned so far and trust that "more will be revealed."

GOD, FOR TODAY, help me to retain and use my sense of humor to successfully finish this chapter of my life.

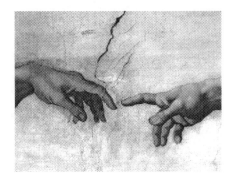

GOD, FOR TODAY, give me the courage to take the steps I need to take to protect myself from the irrational behavior of my partner. I realize he is ill, but if his ship is going down, I know that I don't have to go down with it.

I am still the most valuable dog, and I *know* how to survive.

GOD, FOR TODAY, help me to step out of my own life long enough to look around and *see* the others who are struggling as I have struggled. I know that each of us can do our part, however small, to carry the message to those who still suffer.

GOD, FOR TODAY, give me the strength to stand up to the splitting/ devaluation behavior of my partner.

Help me to feel Your presence surrounding me, deflecting the raging words away from me like a shield of armor. My heart is tender and needs protection.

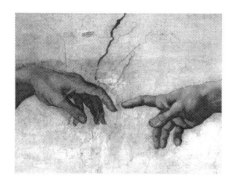

GOD, FOR TODAY, help me to trust that doors are opening and closing for me as is needed for my journey. I know that if the Plan A I thought was happening in my life becomes a closed door, Plan B is already in place. I have only to look for the open door and step through it.

G OD, FOR TODAY, help me to lay down my blaming of myself for being in a painful relationship and the sense of *not being worthy* that I sometimes feel. I know that You love me and that many other people love me also.

I am loved because I have so deeply given love first. The fact that the quality of my love hasn't been returned to me by my BPD partner in the same way I gave it is not my fault.

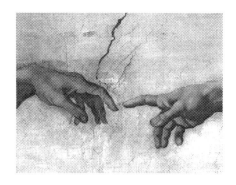

G OD, FOR TODAY, help me to play the *Blame Game* without getting pulled into *dodge ball*. Whether or not my BPD *ever* gets well, the continual blaming erodes my self-esteem and eventually leaves me feeling helpless. I don't want to slip down that far, nor do I deserve it.

Help me find the words to show the love and acceptance I have in my heart for my partner, but also deliver the message that I am *not* responsible for his feelings or actions.

GOD, FOR TODAY, I am grateful to be one of those fortunate ones who have the knowledge to set themselves free. I pray for those still in the dark about the stench they can smell but have no name for.

GOD, FOR TODAY, I ask for courage and strength for myself to enable me to walk through whatever stage of grief I'm in. I trust that forgiveness will be a natural step I take sometime in the future – when I'm able.

GOD, FOR TODAY, help me begin just one new activity that feels good to me. Help me to find the courage to say to a friend, "I need a hug today." I am entirely ready to begin gently and lovingly caring for *myself*, whether my BPD partner begins work on his *own* recovery or not.

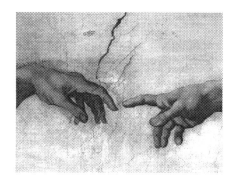

GOD, FOR TODAY, help me to remember that new ways of thinking and acting take time and energy to learn. Help me to withhold judgment as my BPD partner struggles to retrain himself in more effective life skills. Keeping my eyes trained on myself and what I can do to change *my* character flaws would be a good way to show support to my partner.

G OD, FOR TODAY, help me to remember when I'm slipping into depression and pity that things could be much, much worse. I could still be one of the millions of people who don't know the *name of their pain.*

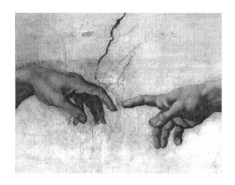

GOD, FOR TODAY, help me to face the reality of how my childhood experiences formed me into the Perfect Partner to the BPD. As my BPD partner works on healing and not using manipulation on me, help me, in turn, learn not to be *manipulatable*.

I know that I can't be abandoned anymore. I am an adult now.

GOD, FOR TODAY, help me be kind to myself as I look at the reality of my deep feelings of betrayal. Help me to remind myself that I did the best I could with the knowledge I had at the time.

Now that I have the knowledge I've needed all along, I can make better choices.

When I know better, I do better.

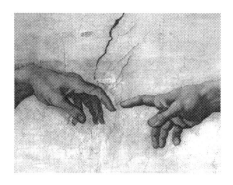

GOD, FOR TODAY, help me to be aware of the subtle signs that I may possibly be blindly walking into yet another BPD relationship. Help me to *see* what I need to see and *hear* what I need to hear. I don't ever want to hurt that bad again.

GOD, FOR TODAY, I am so very grateful for all I'm learning – about BPD and myself. I am being given the key to mastery over *the pain with no name* in my life. Thank you, thank you, thank you.

GOD, FOR TODAY, help me to put my fear aside over whether my relationship will end if I *prepare* for BPD behavior. Putting a shield around myself to protect me from further hurt, stress, and physical and emotional illness is my main priority now. I *must* survive this relationship so I can go on to help the others who still don't know the *name of their pain* or how to protect themselves from it.

God, FOR TODAY, I want to allow my sense of humor out to play. Living with a BPD can drain me of all laughter and joy. Every once in a while, it just plain feels good to have some fun.

GOD, FOR TODAY, show me that I am *not* in "a universe that cares nothing" for my hopes and fears. Besides my spiritual life, bring those people into my life who *do* care about me and support my journey.

Help me to continue measuring and monitoring the progress of my BPD relationship. I want to see clearly when I am becoming a martyr, so I can take action. Remind me that "emancipation, wisdom and charity" and "the birth of a new life" will be my gifts at the end of my struggle with darkness, whether I stay with my BPD partner or not.

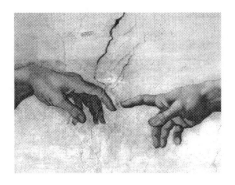

GOD, FOR TODAY, give me the wisdom to see clearly my life and the direction I'm going. And give me the courage to run away if I need to.

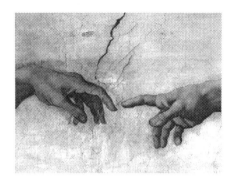

GOD, FOR TODAY, I want to be aware of my "heart condition." If I'm starting to lose my openness and ability to reach out in love to the world around me, perhaps it's time for a reality check regarding how my BPD relationship is affecting me. Help me to perceive my life without denial or minimizing. Help me to know when it's time to leave.

My "heart health" depends on it.

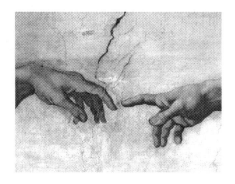

GOD, FOR TODAY, give me the strength to keep my fingers in the dike of my psyche. Help me to shore up my defenses against destructive BPD treatment. Help me to remember who I really am, with all of my good qualities.

I'm doing all that I can to understand this disorder and support my partner as he tries to recover ... but in my heart of hearts, I long to be treated as a Ten-Cow Person. I deserve it.

GOD, FOR TODAY, help me to know in my heart that my struggles are not without purpose. One day, I will look back and see the beautiful tapestry that has been woven out of my tears and broken dreams. I will be surprisingly grateful for the pain of my past and not want to change it.

It's hard to see right now, but I trust it will happen.

GOD, FOR TODAY, help me to know when it's time to jump from my sinking ship relationship and give me the courage and the strength to do so. I trust that Your life preservers and rescue boats are on the way.

GOD, FOR TODAY, help me to open my mind to yet another *theory* regarding why my life is in such chaos. I've read so much and tried so hard … sometimes it just seems hopeless.

One thing I *do* know, though: I *deserve* a happy and joyous life. If my BPD partner isn't going to do *his* part, it's entirely up to me. I may be digging out with a spoon, but eventually, I *will* get out.

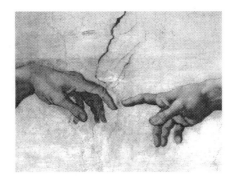

GOD, FOR TODAY, help me to find the medical and mental health professionals who truly understand the nature of this disorder which imprisons me and my family. I long for love, laughter and happiness. I'll pull my covered wagons along whatever path I'm shown, to find the peace I so desire.

GOD, FOR TODAY, help me to hold my head high and not feel ashamed of how my life has become such an embarrassing experience. At least now I know the truth and the *name of my pain*. I can now begin putting the pieces of my life back together again ... with or without my BPD partner. But I *will* get my life back.

GOD, FOR TODAY, help me to do what I can to protect myself and my family – emotionally, physically and financially. I'm struggling to reach a balance between being supportive of my partner while also creating a safe environment for us.

I'm sometimes not sure it's possible, but I'm trying.

GOD, FOR TODAY, give me the strength to just do one thing for myself that warms my heart and nurtures my soul. I want to turn around the downslide I'm in and make it an *upslide*.

GOD, FOR TODAY, help me to feel Your presence in my life. Soothe me as I attempt to quell my fears and make healthy choices for myself. Give me courage as I take my first baby steps in learning to stand up for myself. Help my head to overcome my demon fears and my overly forgiving heart.

GOD, FOR TODAY, help me remember to be gentle with myself as I make this journey. I know what I'm working on now. Learning Who I Am as a loving human being in Your world is a lifetime goal.

RED FLAGS

Red Flags

How did we get into these painful relationships? What signs did we miss that would have tipped us off about our partner's serious emotional problems? We all know *now*, looking backwards, when the particular behaviors began to surface, but could we have seen the *tip of the iceberg* behavior sooner?

The following is a series of insights I've collected from various sources.

A quote from a college professor:

> This is my favorite area of study in all of abnormal psychology. Why? There are two considerations: first, they are not psychotic, hallucinating, falling-down drunk or brain-damaged in most cases; they masquerade as normal humans. Second, they do not feel that anything is wrong with their attitudes or behavior, so they drive ordinary people crazy ... they are *carriers* of stress so severe that it can led to a variety of Axis I diagnoses in loved ones. These people may be your mother, father, in-laws, nieces, nephews, aunts, cousins, friends, lovers, or neighbors. You have no idea that there is anything wrong, as long as you keep your distance psychologically. The instant that you become intimate with a person with one of the Personality Disorders, your reality will shift until you begin to wonder what is wrong with you.

When I teach Personality Disorders, I think of it as a public service announcement – "This is what a person with XXX Personality Disorder is like; if your fiancé acts like this, give the ring back."

People with Personality Disorders sometimes decompensate and are eligible for an Axis I diagnosis such as anxiety disorder, mood disorder, alcoholism, or sexual deviation.

It is unlikely that a person with purely Axis II disorder will ever present for diagnosis or therapy on his own. This person is brought into therapy by the courts, a spouse, or employer unless he or she decompensates so badly that the person seeks out treatment for an Axis I disorder that is causing fairly extreme anguish.

All of the Personality Disorders have a quality of selfishness that you would expect in a child of about five or six; this means that a person with this type of disorder cannot have a reciprocal relationship with an adult, even if their behavior looks selfless.

People with Personality Disorders also make the same mistakes over and over, so that with time, one can see that they resist learning from past experience; everything that happens to them is *not* their fault.

From *Character Disorder* by J. Kent Griffiths, DSW, who says, "We all have several of these traits on a bad day, but if you see a preponderance of these attributes in yourself or the person you're worried about, it may indicate what is called a personality or character disorder. We should work on overcoming these attributes and avoid people who possess many of them."

- Emotional immaturity. Behavior is not age appropriate.
- Self-centeredness. He comes first and foremost. Is insincere about real interest in other people.
- Little if any remorse for mistakes
- Poor judgment
- Unreliability, undependability, irresponsibility
- Inability to profit from experience – does not learn a lesson from making mistakes
- Inability to postpone immediate gratification – what he wants, he wants now. Impulsive and demanding
- Conflict with, or defiance of, authority
- Lack of appreciation for the consequences of his actions
- Tendency to project his own shortcomings on to the world about him – frequent blaming. Never at fault
- Little if any conscience
- Behavior develops little sense of direction – often uninfluenced by concepts of right and wrong
- Gives lip service to professed values and beliefs
- Often involved with illegal or unethical acts
- Shallow interpersonal skills – inability to experience and verbalize deep feelings and emotions. Often insensitive to the needs and feelings of others. Cannot identify with how others feel.

- Ability to put up a good *front* to impress and exploit others
- Low stress tolerance with explosive behavior
- Can *con* to get what he wants to meet his needs, often at the expense of others. The behavior is highly repetitious and many people are used.
- Sees others as pawns on the chess board. Maneuvers people around for his own purposes. When done with them, they are *checkmated* or rejected.
- Ready rationalization – rarely at a loss for words – twists conversation to divorce himself from responsibility
- When he is trapped, he just keeps talking or changes the subject, or gets angry.
- Incapable of maintaining genuine loyalties to any person, group, or code
- Chronic lying
- Does/did poorly in school with attendance, grades, attitudes, and relationships with teachers. Was in conflict with parents over school performance.
- *Chip on shoulder* attitude – cocky and arrogant
- Rebellious to parents' authority. Violates standards of the home frequently.
- Cancels commitments without sound reason or warning.
- Uses friends for money, transportation, favors, time, attention, etc.
- A taker – not a giver. Gives for show but expects something in return.
- Glimpses of integrity and emotion are seen – but short lived. Gives you hope he's changing, but returns soon to deviant behavior.
- Lives life of avoiding responsibility vs. getting the job done.
- Poor self-motivation – often described as lazy and listless. Lacks ambition. Not helpful with routine chores.
- Fun is the cornerstone of his life.
- Sexually curious or active. Places great importance on his sexual abilities. Female sexual partner often feels used and demanded of.
- Lacks well-defined values.
- Comes across initially as caring and understanding and reads others "like a book" because he makes his business knowing how to maneuver people.

- In a trust relationship, inevitably betrays and violates the commitments and gets blocked emotionally when gets too close to those he says he loves.

- Angry mood most of the time.

- Uses sex to control, cover his insecurity or make up after a fight.

- Has no concept of open sharing of ideas, feelings, emotions. Conversation goes per his direction. He has the last word always. He determines how, when, where we talk, and about what he wants to talk about.

- Can show real tenderness of feeling, then return to customary behaviors. Two (or more) vastly different sides to his personality are seen.

- Poor planner with time and activity

- Is very slow to forgive others. Hangs on to resentment.

- Excessively concerned with personal appearance; e.g., hair, weight, car he drives, clothes, having money to flash, career dreaming

- Seems to enjoy disturbing others. Likes to agitate and disrupt for no apparent reason.

- Feels entitled to the *good life* without working for it.

- He never seems to get enough of what he wants. He leaves others drained and confused.

- Others get upset when in his presence. There's a feeling of guardedness, caution, and suspicion that he creates in others.

- Moody – switches from nice guy to anger without much provocation.

- Poor work history – quitting, being fired, interpersonal conflicts

- Repeatedly fails to honor financial obligations. Does not pay the bills in a responsible and timely way.

- Unable to sustain a totally faithful relationship with loved one of the opposite sex.

- Flirtatious, overly friendly. Makes inappropriate sexual comments to/about other women.

- Seldom expresses appreciation. Again, is thinking of his needs vs. the needs of others.

- Grandiose. Convinced that he knows more than other people and is correct and right in almost all he says and does.

- Clueless as to how he comes across to others and to how he is viewed. Gets defensive when confronted with his behavior. Never his fault. May be apologetic and seem sincere, but soon repeats offensive behavior without appearing to have learned from it.
- Motive for behavior is usually self-serving, and he does not recognize it.
- Can get very emotional, even tearful, but behavior is more about show or frustration rather than contrition or sorrow.
- He breaks women's spirits to keep them dependent.
- Survives on threats, intimidations to keep others chained to him.
- Sabotages anything that makes his spouse/girlfriend happy. Wants her to be happy only through him and to have few/no outside interests/friends/family.
- Highly contradictory. He loves me, he hates me. He threatens me with poverty, then indulges me or our relationship.
- He is always working somebody over – either subtly or aggressively for a favor, deal, break, freebie, discount, etc.
- Double standard. He is free to do his thing, but expects others to be what he wants them to be/do. He doesn't let others be themselves.
- Convincing. Successful at getting other people to believe in his perception of a problem. Is adamant that people side with him vs. allowing them to feel/believe differently.
- Hides who he really is from everyone. No one really knows the real him.
- Scorns everyone/everything that he disagrees with. Does not allow for differences to be respected. Scorns the responsible world.
- Difficult to pin him down to a certain level of integrity that you can live with. Resists all efforts to define his values, behaviors, standards.
- Kind to you usually only if he's getting from you what he wants.
- He has to be right. He has to win. He has to look good.
- He announces, not discusses. He tells, not asks.
- He does not discuss openly beforehand. You get to deal with *after the fact* information.

- Controls money of others but spends freely on himself and others.
- You end up feeling responsible for the problem. He gets to your feelings. No matter what, he wins, you lose.
- He wins at the expense of your feelings. Thinks only of the end result without considering your feelings or needs in the process.
- Attitude of "I'll meet your needs if you meet mine. If you don't, I'll find someone else who will or I will not meet yours."
- Unilateral condition of, "I'm OK and justified, so I don't need to hear your position or ideas."
- Does not take responsibility for his behavior.
- The hurt he describes is because he got caught, or he's mad that you're mad, and not because he believes he made a mistake.
- Secret life. You're often wondering what he does or who he is that you don't know about.
- Always feels misunderstood.
- Most of the time you feel miserable living with this person. When it's good, you relish the peace, but that is usually short lived.
- He is so skilled at making a mountain out of a molehill, and you become so tired of the conflict. It drains all of your energy, love and hope.
- Is usually through listening once he's made his arguments.
- We talk about his feelings, not mine.
- Unchallenged by people because they seem to be put off by him, afraid of him, or he eludes them.
- Is not interested in problem-solving openly.
- Seems very interested in discerning personalities, so that he can strategize how to manipulate them.

Finally, Dear Abby chimes in with her list of signs to tip us off to a potential abuser:

DEAR ABBY: The letter from "At My Wit's End," whose best friend's husband was insanely jealous, prompted me to write.

For 13 years, I was married to a very controlling, much older man. A woman named "Helen" from church would call me occasionally. Since I wasn't allowed to have friends, each time she called, my husband would make a scene in the background. I was extremely embarrassed, but one day, she said: "He's trying to run me off. He may have been in your life a long time before me, but I'll be around long after he's gone!"

That statement caused me to review my situation and realize the extent to which I was being controlled. Suddenly, I experienced a feeling of power where before I felt helpless. I came to realize that I was miserable in my marriage, but I had believed it was all my fault. Had it not been for Helen's comment, I might still be in that abusive relationship (which it was).

That was 20 years ago. I divorced him, and my life has changed tremendously since then. Please, Abby, tell "Wit's End" she may be her friend's only link to a new life.

– Been There in Texas

DEAR BEEN THERE: I'll do better than that. I'll point out that being isolated from friends and family by a partner – male or female – is one sign of a potential abuser. Read on for some other signs (adapted with permission from the Project for Victims of Family Violence in Fayetteville, Ark.), any one of which could be a sign of abuse.

- PUSHES FOR QUICK INVOLVEMENT: Comes on strong, claiming, "I've never felt loved like this by anyone." An abuser pressures the new partner for an exclusive commitment almost immediately.

- JEALOUS: Excessively possessive; calls constantly or visits unexpectedly; prevents you from going to work because "you might meet someone"; checks the mileage on your car.

- CONTROLLING: Interrogates you intensely (especially if you're late) about whom you talked to and where you were; keeps all the money; insists you ask permission to go anywhere or do anything.

- UNREALISTIC EXPECTATIONS: Expects you to be the perfect mate and meet his or her every need.

- ISOLATION: Tries to cut you off from family and friends; accuses people who are your supporters of "causing trouble." The abuser may deprive you of a phone or car, or try to prevent you from holding a job.

- BLAMES OTHERS FOR PROBLEMS OR MISTAKES: It's always someone else's fault if something goes wrong.

- MAKES OTHERS RESPONSIBLE FOR HIS OR HER FEELINGS: The abuser says, "You make me angry," instead of, "I am angry," or says, "You're hurting me by not doing what I tell you."

- HYPERSENSITIVITY: Is easily insulted, claiming hurt feelings when he or she is really mad. Rants about the injustice of things that are just a part of life.

- CRUELTY TO ANIMALS AND CHILDREN: Kills or punishes animals brutally. Also, may expect children to do things that are far beyond their ability (whips a three-year-old for wetting a diaper), or may tease them until they cry. Sixty-five per cent of abusers who beat their partner will also abuse children.

- "PLAYFUL" USE OF FORCE DURING SEX: Enjoys throwing you down or holding you down against your will during sex; finds the idea of rape exciting.

- VERBAL ABUSE: Constantly criticizes or says blatantly cruel, hurtful things; degrades, curses, calls you ugly names. This may also involve sleep deprivation, waking you up with relentless verbal abuse.

- RIGID SEX ROLES: Expects you to serve, obey, stay at home.

- SUDDEN MOOD SWINGS: Switches from sweet to violent in minutes.

- PAST BATTERING: Admits to hitting a mate in the past, but says the person "made" him (or her) do it.

- THREATS OF VIOLENCE: Says things like, "I'll break your neck," or "I'll kill you," and then dismisses them with, "Everybody talks that way," or "I didn't really mean it." If the abuse has gone this far – it's time to get help or get out!

Definitions and Behavior Descriptions of Borderline and Narcissistic Personality Disorders

Definitions and Behavior Descriptions of Borderline and Narcissistic Personality Disorders

How do we describe how a BPD acts? How can we put it all into just one nutshell description when BPDs come in so many different shapes, sizes, colors and flavors?

Some explode in rages. Some lurk quietly in the background and then attack. Others withdraw for days, weeks ... months. Some control the actions of their partner, even stalking them. There are signs of depression, to the point of attempting suicide sometimes.

Some do all of the above. The list seems endless, twisting and turning the BPD's partner as each new behavior is exhibited.

How do we describe to others the *never knowing* from one minute to the next whether they'll explode at us? How can we tell people how nervous we feel when it gets *quiet?* Are they withdrawing and building up steam for a volcano act? Or are they quietly watching *us*, looking for signs that *we* are leaving?

How do we describe the feeling of having a ticking time bomb in our own home – our supposed-to-be-*safe* place? It feels so hopeless sometimes.

In its second and third DSM editions, the American Psychiatric Association added to its list of criterion for mental illnesses ten types of personality/character disorders, all of which result in significant distress and/or negative consequences within the individual. This information was updated in its Diagnostic and Statistical Manual of Mental Disorders, Fourth Edition (DSM-IV), Washington, D. C.: American Psychiatric Association, 1994, pp. 650 – 654.

The reader can do additional research to learn about the other eight personality disorders, but in *Breaking Free from Boomerang Love*, the two personality disorders of borderline personality disorder and narcissism are the focal points. Speaking about borderline personality disorder without including narcissism would present an incomplete picture.

Therefore, included below are descriptions of both the borderline personality disorder and the narcissistic personality disorder.

BORDERLINE PERSONALITY DISORDER

Excellent web sites for additional information about borderline personality disorder are www.ybrt.org, www.tara4bpd.org., www.mentalhealth-today.com, and www.borderlineresearch.org.

DSM-IV

According to the DSM-IV, persons with borderline personality disorder display a pervasive pattern of instability of interpersonal relationships, self-image, and affects and marked impulsivity beginning by early adulthood and present in a variety of contexts, as indicated by five (or more) of the following:

1. Frantic efforts to avoid real or imagined abandonment. (Note: Do not include suicidal or self-mutilating behavior covered in Criterion 5.)

2. A pattern of unstable and intense interpersonal relationships characterized by alternating between extremes of idealization and devaluation

3. Identity disturbance: markedly and persistently unstable self-image or sense of self

4. Impulsivity in at least two areas that are potentially self-damaging (e.g., spending, sex, substance abuse, reckless driving, binge eating). (Note: Do not include suicidal or self-mutilating behavior covered in Criterion 5.)

5. Recurrent suicidal behavior, gestures, or threats, or self-mutilating behavior

6. Affective instability due to a marked reactivity of mood (e.g., intense episodic dysphoria, irritability, or anxiety usually lasting a few hours and only rarely more than a few days

7. Chronic feelings of emptiness

8. Inappropriate, intense anger or difficulty controlling anger (e.g., frequent displays of temper, constant anger, recurrent physical fights)

9. Transient, stress-related paranoid ideation or severe dissociative symptoms.

The DSM-IV goes on to say:

The essential feature of Borderline Personality Disorder is a pervasive pattern of instability of interpersonal relationships, self-image, and affects, and marked impulsivity that begins by early adulthood and is present in a variety of contexts.

Individuals with Borderline Personality Disorder make frantic efforts to avoid real or imagined abandonment (Criterion 1). The perception of impending separation or rejection, or the loss of external structure, can lead to profound changes in self-image, affect, cognition, and behavior. These individuals are very sensitive to environmental circumstances. They experience intense abandonment fears and inappropriate anger even when faced with a realistic time-limited separation or when there are unavoidable changes in plans (e.g., sudden despair in reaction to a clinician's announcing the end of the hour; panic or fury when someone important to them is just a few minutes late or must cancel an appointment). They may believe that this "abandonment" implies they are "bad". These abandonment fears are related to an intolerance of being alone and a need to have other people with them. Their frantic efforts to avoid abandonment may include impulsive action such as self-mutilating or suicidal behaviors, which are described separately in Criterion 5.

Individuals with Borderline Personality Disorder have a pattern of unstable and intense relationships (Criterion 2). They may idealize potential caregivers or lovers at the first or second meeting, demand to spend a lot of time together, and share the most intimate details early in a relationship. However, they may switch quickly from idealizing other people to devaluing them, feeling that the other person does not care enough, does not give enough, is not "there" enough. These individuals can empathize with and nurture other people, but only with the expectation that the other person will "be there" in return to meet their own needs on demand. These individuals are prone to sudden and dramatic shifts in their view of others, who may alternately be seen as beneficent supports or as cruelly punitive. Such shifts often reflect disillusionment with a caregiver whose nurturing qualities had been idealized or whose rejection or abandonment is expected.

There may be an identity disturbance characterized by markedly and persistently unstable self-image or sense of self (Criterion 3). There are sudden and dramatic shifts in self-image, characterized by shifting goals, values, and vocational aspirations. There may be sudden changes in opinions and plans about career, sexual identity, values, and types of friends. These individuals may suddenly change from the role of a needy supplicant for help to a righteous avenger of past mistreatment. Although they usually have a self-image that is based on being bad or evil, individuals with this disorder may at times have feelings that they do not exist at all. Such experiences usually occur in situations in which the individual feels a lack of meaningful relationship, nurturing and support. These individuals may show worse performance in unstructured work or school situations.

Individuals with this disorder display impulsivity in at least two areas that are potentially self-damaging (Criterion 4). They may gamble, spend money irresponsibly, binge eat, abuse substances, engage in unsafe sex, or drive recklessly.

Individuals with Borderline Personality Disorder display recurrent suicidal behavior, gestures, or threats, or self-mutilating behavior (Criterion 5). Completed suicide occurs in eight to ten per cent of such individuals, and self-mutilative acts (e.g., cutting or burning) and suicide threats and attempts are very common. Recurrent suicidality is often the reason that these individuals present for help. These self-destructive acts are usually precipitated by threats of separation or rejection or by expectations that they assume increased responsibility. Self-mutilation may occur during dissociative experiences and often brings relief by reaffirming the ability to feel or by expiating the individual's sense of being evil.

Individuals with Borderline Personality Disorder may display affective instability that is due to a marked reactivity of mood (e.g., intense episodic dysphoria, irritability, or anxiety usually lasting few hours and only rarely more than a few days) (Criterion 6). The basic dysphoric mood of those with borderline personality disorder is often disrupted by periods of anger, panic, or despair and is rarely relieved by periods of well-being or satisfaction.

These episodes may reflect the individual's extreme reactivity troubled by chronic feelings of emptiness (Criterion 7). Easily bored, they may constantly seek something to do.

Individuals with Borderline Personality Disorder frequently express inappropriate, intense anger or have difficulty controlling their anger (Criterion 8). They may display extreme sarcasm, enduring bitterness, or verbal outbursts. The anger is often elicited when a caregiver or lover is seen as neglectful, withholding, uncaring, or abandoning. Such expression of anger are often followed by shame and guilt and contribute to the feeling they have of being evil.

During periods of extreme stress, transient paranoid ideation or dissociative symptoms (e.g., depersonalization) may occur (Criterion 9), but these are generally of insufficient severity or duration to warrant an additional diagnosis. These episodes occur most frequently in response to a real or imagined abandonment. Symptoms tend to be transient, lasting minutes or hours. The real or perceived return of the caregiver's nurturance may result in a remission of symptoms.

Associated Features and Disorders

Individuals with Borderline Personality Disorder may have a pattern of undermining themselves at the moment a goal is about to be realized (e.g., dropping out of school just before graduation; regressing severely after a discussion of how well therapy is going; destroying a good relationship just when it is clear that the relationship could last). Some individuals develop psychotic-like symptoms (e.g., hallucinations, body-image distortions, ideas of reference, and hypnotic phenomena) during times of stress. Individuals with this disorder may feel more secure with transitional objects (i.e., a pet or inanimate possession) than in interpersonal relationships. Premature death from suicide may occur in individuals with this disorder, especially in those with co-occurring Mood Disorders or Substance-Related Disorders. Physical handicaps may result from self-inflicted abuse behaviors or failed suicide attempts. Recurrent job losses, interrupted education, and broken marriages are common. Physical and sexual abuse, neglect, hostile conflict, and early parental loss or separation are more common in the childhood histories of those with borderline personality disorder. Common co-occurring Axis I disorders include Mood Disorders, Substance-Related Disorders, Eating Disorders (notably Bulimia), Post Traumatic Stress Disorder, and Attention-Deficit/Hyperactivity Disorder. Borderline Personality Disorder also frequently co-occurs with other Personality Disorders.

Specific Culture, Age, and Gender Features

The pattern of behavior seen in Borderline Personality Disorder has been identified in many settings around the world. Adolescents and young adults with identity problems (especially when accompanied by substance abuse) may transiently display behaviors that misleadingly give the impression of Borderline Personality Disorder. Such situations are characterized by emotional instability, "existential" dilemmas, uncertainty, anxiety-provoking choices, conflicts about sexual orientation, and competing social pressures to decide on careers.

Borderline Personality Disorder is diagnosed predominantly (about 75 per cent) in females.

Prevalence

The prevalence of Borderline Personality Disorder is estimated to be about two per cent of the general population, about ten per cent among individuals seen in outpatient mental health clinics, and about 20 per cent among psychiatric inpatients. It ranges from 30 per cent to 60 per cent among clinical populations with Personality Disorders.

Course

There is considerable variability in the course of Borderline Personality Disorder. The most common pattern is one of chronic instability in early adulthood, with episodes of serious affective and impulsive dyscontrol and high levels of use of health and mental health resources. The impairment from the disorder and the risk of suicide are greatest in the young adult years and gradually wane with advancing age. During their 30's and 40's, the majority of individuals with this disorder attain greater stability in their relationships and vocational functioning.

Familial Pattern

Borderline Personality Disorder is about five times more common among first-degree biological relatives of those with the disorder than in the general population. There is also an increased familial risk for Substance-Related Disorders, Antisocial Personality Disorder, and Mood Disorders.

Differential Diagnosis

Borderline Personality Disorder often co-occurs with Mood Disorders, and when criteria for both are met, both may be diagnosed. Because the cross-sectional presentation of Borderline Personality Disorder can be mimicked by an episode of Mood Disorder, the clinician should avoid giving an additional diagnosis of Borderline Personality Disorder based only on cross-sectional presentation without having documented that the pattern of behavior has an early onset and a long-standing course.

Other Personality Disorders may be confused with Borderline Personality Disorder because they have certain features in common. It is, therefore, important to distinguish among these disorders based on differences in their characteristic features. However, if an individual has personality features that meet criteria for one or more Personality Disorders in addition to Borderline Personality Disorder, all can be diagnosed.

Although Histrionic Personality Disorder can also be characterized by attention seeking, manipulative behavior, and rapidly shifting emotions, Borderline Personality Disorder is distinguished by self-destructiveness, angry disruptions in close relationships, and chronic feelings of deep emptiness and loneliness.

Paranoid ideas or illusions may be present in both Borderline Personality Disorder and Schizotypal Personality Disorder, but these symptoms are more transient, interpersonally reactive, and responsive to external structuring in Borderline Personality Disorder.

Although Paranoid Personality Disorder and Narcissistic Personality Disorder may also be characterized by an angry reaction to minor stimuli, the relative stability of self-image as well as the relative lack of self-destructiveness, impulsivity, and abandonment concerns distinguish these disorders from Borderline Personality Disorder.

Although Antisocial Personality Disorder and Borderline Personality Disorder are both characterized by manipulative behavior, individuals with Antisocial Personality Disorder are manipulative to gain profit, power, or some other material gratification, whereas the goal in Borderline Personality Disorder is directed more toward gaining the concern of caretakers.

Both Dependent Personality Disorder and Borderline Personality Disorder are characterized by fear of abandonment. However, the individual with Borderline Personality Disorder reacts to abandonment with feelings of emotional emptiness, rage, and demands, whereas the individual with Dependent Personality Disorder reacts with increasing appeasement and submissiveness and urgently seeks a replacement relationship to provide care giving and support. Borderline Personality Disorder can further be distinguished from Dependent Personality Disorder by the typical pattern of unstable and intense relationships.

NARCISSISTIC PERSONALITY DISORDER

Dr. Sam Vaknin's web site http://malignantselflove.tripod.com is an excellent source for additional information about narcissism.

The common traits of narcissism can be distilled as follows:
- An obvious self-focus in interpersonal exchanges
- Problems in sustaining satisfying relationships
- Lack of psychological awareness
- Difficulty with empathy
- Problems distinguishing the self from others
- Hypersensitivity to any slights or imagined insults
- Lack of emotional depth and ability to feel sadness; and vulnerability to shame rather than guilt.

According to the DSM-IV, display of five of the following nine behaviors certifies a person as having narcissistic personality disorder:
- Feels grandiose and self-important – Exaggerates achievements and talents to the point of lying; demands to be recognized as superior without commensurate achievements
- Is obsessed with fantasies of unlimited success, fame, fearsome power or omnipotence, unequalled brilliance (the cerebral narcissist), bodily beauty or sexual performance (the somatic narcissist), or ideal, everlasting, all-conquering love or passion
- Firmly convinced that he or she is unique and, being special, can only be understood by, should only be treated by, or associate with, other special or unique, or high-status people (or institutions)

- Requires excessive admiration, adulation, attention and affirmation – or, failing that, wishes to be feared and to be notorious (narcissistic supply)
- Feels entitled. Expects unreasonable or special and favorable priority treatment.
- Demands automatic and full compliance with his or her expectations
- Is interpersonally exploitative – uses others to achieve his or her own ends
- Devoid of empathy. Is unable or unwilling to identify with or acknowledge the feelings and needs of others
- Constantly envious of others or believes that they feel the same about him or her
- Arrogant, haughty behaviors or attitudes coupled with rage when frustrated, contradicted, or confronted.

Quick Order Form

NAME: _____

ADDRESS: _____

_____

CITY, STATE, ZIP: _____

PLEASE SEND THE FOLLOWING BOOKS:

TITLE: PRICE:

_____

_____

SALES TAX: CA RESIDENTS ADD 7.5%: _____

SHIPPING BY AIR (SEE RATES BELOW): _____

GRAND TOTAL:_____

SHIPPING RATES:
U.S.: $4.00 FOR FIRST BOOK; $2.00 FOR EACH ADDITIONAL
INTERNATIONAL: $9.00 FOR FIRST BOOK; $5.00 FOR EACH ADDITIONAL

SEND ORDER FORM AND CHECK/MONEY ORDER
TO: MELVILLE PUBLICATIONS, P.O. BOX 2036,
SANTA MARIA, CA 93457-2036
OR ORDER VIA THE WEBSITE: www.boomeranglove.com

Enter email address to receive notice of future books, appearances, and breaking news about BPD:

_____

Printed in the United States
87184LV00003B/142-150/A

9 780976 060048